Wisdom, Magic, Miracles and More

Learning Life's Lessons Before It's Too Late

By S. C. Klane

Wisdom, Magic, Miracles and More
Learning Life's Lessons Before It's Too Late

Published by JingotheCat.com
Book designed by Andy Grachuk

Forward

May the sun bring you new energy by day,
may the moon softly restore you by night,
may the rain wash away your worries,
may the breeze blow new strength into your being,
may you walk gently through the world and
know it's beauty all the days of your life.

~Apache Blessing

Preface

Hello, and thank you for buying <u>Wisdom, Magic, Miracles and More.</u> <u>Learning Life's Lessons Before It's Too Late</u>.

First, I would like to point out that this book is created by me, but it is not mine. I owe it all to my creator and all the teachers by whom I am surrounded.

Much like the previous book of Wisdom, this book continues to focus on how important living in the moment is, and how we create suffering for ourselves when we don't. Once again, most of the wisdom in this book I learned from books and spiritual leaders as well as some of my own personal wisdom has been incorporated.

These books always work best when practicing with another person. Ask a friend or family member if he or she would like to get well and become a Zen Master.

I hope this book helps you find Peace, Serenity, and Happiness.

"Keep it in the Moment!"

Stu

"The Grass is Always Greener Where You Water It."

*I*t has been said that the grass is always greener on the other side. Well, that person never tried watering their own lawn.

People think it's easier to dodge life's challenges or jump ship to find a new situation that appears to be problem-free.

Only after watering your own lawn and speaking with your spiritual-adviser, can you then make a decision to move on to your next lawn party.

"Every day is a holiday and every meal is Thanksgiving."

When we awaken to our life's purpose to be here now, this is a cause for celebration.

Why not celebrate each day that has been granted to you?

You don't have to wait for a calendar holiday to surround yourself with friends and loved ones to share traditional food.

Also, you don't have to wait for a calendar holiday to commit a random act of kindness

"The more aware you become, the more conscious you become, the more mindful you become, the more time you will spend in the moment with happiness."

*Y*our life's purpose is to become aware of yourself in this moment. Being consciously aware within each moment will begin the mindful practice of happiness. The human mind, small in capacity has a hard time grasping this concept.

Practice meditating on your breath. Inhaling is receiving and exhaling is giving. Focus on the cool air rushing in and out of your lungs.

Congratulations! You have just returned to the moment. You are now in alignment with the universe. You are now a Zen Master.

Now continue to repeat this process.

"Be a human being, not a human doing."

*I*t seems in today's society most people are all caught up in busy doing.

If you have ever said, "There is not enough time in the day" , or "Everything is crazy right now", then this is for you.

We are called "Human Beings" not "Human Doings."

Pay attention to the "Be" in Beings. Try to "Be" here now. Try to "Be" where your feet are.

Dragging your past around or worrying about the future is a waste of a valuable moment.

When we awaken and stay focused on the "Be" in Being and stop running around looking for salvation in the next moment, we can then allow peace to enter our lives, followed by happiness.

Life is too long to run around like ants on a log, or like scared rabbits.

"If you don't arrest your mind, you will be the one who goes to prison."

One of people's biggest problems is "mindless obsessive thinking."

Don't be a victim of unorganized thinking. This is one of the core roots of what's driving people crazy and has been for thousands of years.

Take a step back from the madness and concentrate on what you are thinking about. Become aware of your words and actions.

Peace of mind can only happen when you have peace in your moment.

"It's not so much trying to control your mind as it is trying not to let your mind control you."

*D*id you know that most people suffer from some kind of obsessive compulsive behavior in one form or another?

First, we must become aware of our thought patterns and then we can become aware of our compulsive behavior that can be destructive and create suffering.

Check in with yourself and ask if you are doing a particular action without your permission.

Only by becoming aware of our thought patterns followed by destructive behavior, can we then bring our minds back to the present moment and begin creating positive thought patterns followed by positive actions.

You can achieve anything you want if you want peace and happiness bad enough.

"Your life is only as complicated as your mind allows it to be."

Not living in the present moment can create a complicated busy mind.

Many people, places and things are constantly tugging at you to take you out of the moment. This can create a mind-made "Category Five" hurricane.

Take a step back out of your hectic moment. Practice single-tasking and create new boundaries for people who are known "moment wreckers."

If someone asks you what you are doing this weekend, or for Christmas, it's okay to tell them, "I don't know. I'm trying to stay focused on today." After awhile they will stop asking you questions.

"Ego stands for: 'Everybody's Got One.'"

Some people believe that Ego means that someone is better than someone else. Well it does, and so much more.

Ego is the ultimate attacher. It loves to attach itself to people, places and things----good, bad or indifferent.

It loves to attach itself to names, job titles, cars, boats, and feeling superior and inferior toward other people. It's solely responsible for the seven deadly sins of pride, greed, lust, envy, gluttony, wrath and sloth. So as you can see, it is so much more than you think.

Try being your true authentic self in the moment with no fake disguises and no ulterior motives.

"One of the most selfish things you can do is have an anxiety attack."

When people are suffering from an anxiety attack they are playing a movie in their mind of worst case scenarios creating fear, or they are playing old movies of unfortunate situations and are fearful that these things could happen again.

The truth is that these things that are being thought about are not happening "now."

It only feels as if they are. Remember, feelings are not facts. Obsessive, compulsive thinking about yourself is a selfish act which will get you nowhere except a visit to the local psyche ward.

Become aware of your compulsive need to think only of yourself and reverse the curse today. Lots of therapy and group meetings are a great remedy followed by helping people less fortunate than you.

Contrary to your belief, there are a lot of people less fortunate than you.

"The plan for the future is to be here now."

*A*re you tired of being "sick and tired"? Are you tired of dragging your past around like bags of heavy luggage with no wheels or retractable handles? Are you ready to stop playing worst case scenarios of the future? Are you finally going to stop worrying that you are "not enough", and don't have enough today, or for when you retire?

The only remedy to fix these mind viruses is to stay in the present moment, here and now. No pill, drink, or shopping spree will heal these viruses. We have all proved this theory.

Dare to team together with a group of people who are "sick and tired of being sick and tired." Start practicing staying present in the moment with positivity and gratitude.

Peace of mind and happiness await you.

"We are spiritual beings having a human experience."

*B*eing a human being with all character flaws and emotions, good and bad, can keep us on an emotional roller coaster ride.

The most important thing to focus on is not to take life so seriously.

Remember, "Don't sweat the small stuff", and it's all "small stuff."

If this were your last day on the planet, is this how you would want to go out?

"Become conscious of your consciousness which is the awareness of your thinking."

*Y*our eyes are open, but more than likely you are not conscious.

Check in with yourself and see if you are consciously aware in this moment. You can only be conscious of your consciousness in this moment. This is the beginning of your awareness of your thought.

Ultimately our goal here and now is to be present in each moment.

This is where the universe lives in the light of consciousness.

"It is impossible to awaken to the moment and anesthetize yourself at the same time."

Many people drink alcohol to have a good time, relax, become chatty, or to take the so-called "edge" off.

Much of the alcohol people drink today is made of the same ingredients surgeons used in the past to sedate patients before surgery, which is why if you drink too much alcohol you eventually pass out.

If you are trying to practice mind, body and spirit, it is important to stay focused in the moment with consciousness.

You can see how it would be impossible to stay conscious while anesthetizing yourself at the same time.

"Wake up organically, not electronically."

*I*t's not by accident that people in the know say how important it is to get eight hours of sleep each night. We need this sacred time to heal all of our organs.

When our eyes open each morning, it is important not to be startled by a loud bell or annoying buzzer. This is because it will cause an adrenaline dump and you will be starting off your day in "fight" or "flight" mode. Also, it is important not to jump right on your phone or computer to start texting, emailing and face-booking.

Be more focused on what you are doing instead of what others are doing.

Dare to put down the electronics and observe your surroundings including nature.

Peace and happiness can be found in the moment and in nature, not on the world wide web.

" Try to be response-able, not react-able."

*I*t is a normal reaction to react to all of life's situations when we come from a family of "rage-aholics" with traumas, dramas, issues, and tissues. This is called conditioned responses, or "monkey-see, monkey-do, monkey get in trouble too."

Instead of acting like the people we swore we would never become, try taking a step back from the situation before snapping and going through the "rage" followed by the "I'm sorry" episode.

Try responding to life's situations and challenges. This is called using your wise mind from your higher self.

"Be eco-friendly, not ego friendly."

*D*id you know that the Earth Mother (your real mother), loves you unconditionally? She provides you with sunlight, moonlight, water, air, and the materials we all need, such as food, clothing, and shelter.

The ego, however, doesn't want you to know how much the earth mother loves you. The ego wants you to take her for granted. That way the ego entices you to put chemicals on your lawns and to avoid recycling properly, contributing to more toxins in the earth and poisoning our water supply.

Although the Earth Mother knows about the ego, she still loves all of her children unconditionally and still does the best job providing everything we need for survival.

Awaken today and make efforts to take better care of our "Earth Mother."

"Listen, or your tongue will keep you deaf."

Have you ever checked in with yourself to see if you are the one who is talking all the time? The reason people do this is because of the ego and nervousness. The ego always wants you to be comparing. It wants you to ask, "Am I better than?" or "Am I less than?"

If you are that person, talking all the time, it is to prove that you have more, know more, or to try to cover up feelings of inferiority, hoping no one will ever find out.

Dare to stop talking, and be the enlightened observer. You might just learn something.

"Do what you can, with what you have, where you are."

Are you chronically unhappy because you don't think that you have everything here and now? Are you constantly looking to the future for happiness and it never comes? Are you always thinking about a geographical cure? Do you think that if you moved to a tropical paradise all your problems would go away?

Well, save your money and a lot of wasted time because you already have everything you need to find long lasting happiness inside of you here and now.

Happiness cannot be found in the material or monetary world. It cannot be found in the future, and it cannot be found in a new place with new people.

You have everything you need to find happiness inside of "you" right here, right now if you would only awaken to it.

"If you spot it you got it."

A lot of people like to put on their black robes and pick up their gavels and start judging people. This is a learned behavior and can be unlearned. This is a deadly virus because you are surrounding yourself with negative energy.

When we are chronically picking people apart because of their character defects and shortcomings, it is because we are suffering from the same things. We are blind to this because of the ego. Awaken to how the ego calls the shots in our lives and blinds us to the things that are most important.

Look to the universe to allow our true light to shine.

*"Magic is when we tell the universe what we want,
Miracles are when we ask the universe what it wants."*

When we awaken to the moment and stop letting the ego call the shots in our life, we will be in alignment with the universe.

This is the part of our lives when dreams come true and we start living our life's purpose. This is the part of our lives when we are satisfied and accept ourselves and our lives this moment. All is okay in this moment. It has always been okay, and it will continue to always be okay.

Because our lives are so good and the hole in our souls have been filled, we can now ask the universe what we can do to return the favor. This is the opposite of self-will.

Transform your life today and realize true balance is to "Give and Take."

"When telling a story, be like a mountain climber,
get to the point."

*S*ome people like to talk and talk, telling every little small detail of every little thing going on in their life, starting with their conception.

The ego wants you to believe that you and your story are the most important things in the universe and every detail is pertinent information.

Dare to awaken to this and understand conversation is a two-way street, both talking and listening.

Become conscious and try to make your stories more like the "Readers Digest" version.

"Cancel your subscription to people with issues."

O nce awakened to doing the right things and thinking correctly, you are going to become aware of why you were the way you were.

You were surrounded by people riddled with mind viruses and negativity. It's okay to stop living with and hanging around family even though you share the same DNA. Also, once awakened you will discover you don't have as much in common with your old high school friends as you thought.

Dare to walk the spiritual road alone so the universe will match you up with positive, spiritual people to hang out with. Watch your whole world change!

"The Earth Mother provides for everyone's needs, but not for everyone's greeds."

One thing we must continue learning about and keeping ourselves in check with is a character defect called "Greed." Greed is among the leading causes of sickness and suffering.

Worrying about whether or not you will have enough down the road is a mind virus you contracted. If you have everything you need today, which is food, clothing, and shelter, there is no reason to believe you will not have everything you need tomorrow. It is fear (false evidence appearing real), that makes people stock-pile and hoard.

Trust and believe and stay focused on today and the moment.

"Awaken to the two gifts our creator gave us to open this morning - our eyes."

When awakening in the morning it is important to start your day on a positive note, asking the creator for guidance and acceptance.

Thank the creator for another day handwritten for us. Become aware of all the gifts that have been given to us by the creator that we have been taking for granted.

Find gratitude in each moment of each day, for this automatically grounds you and turns each moment positive.

"Simple pleasures bring big treasures."

It seems as though in this fast-paced world a lot of people are angry, unhappy, and racing to get to the next moment and place, hoping that they will find what they are looking for.

Perhaps this is the new so-called "American Dream." It's called the "American Dream" because you have to be asleep to enjoy it.

When we are so involved in this complex, complicated, fast-paced living, we are missing out on the simple pleasures of simplicity.

Dare to unleash yourself from your TV, Internet, and traumas, dramas, issues, and tissues. Search for a simpler way of life, similar to back in the old days.

People appeared to be smiling more if you look at any old photos. Let's learn from them.

Remember that your life is only as complicated as you allow it to be.

"If you focus on results, you will never change, but if you focus on change, you will get results."

$\mathcal{I}$ f all you ever do is focus on results, you will be missing out on the journey that takes place one step at a time, one moment at a time.

"The journey of a thousand miles begins with one step." Focus on change in each moment of each step.

Become aware of what you do want this moment, not what you don't want this moment.

Begin to see the magic of change happening in your life to create the results.

"Don't go through life, grow through life."

When people get into routines that they don't necessarily care for each day, they tend to unconsciously go to sleep. Driving to work and not remembering the journey is no way to enjoy your life. Remember that stagnant water breeds malaria.

Instead, dare to make a change so you can start growing through life. Dare to change your current job into a new life's purpose for you. Dare to learn new things and travel to new places. Don't wait until you reach a certain age or until a certain percentage of your pension kicks in. By then it may be too late.

Many people awaken on their death bed and wonder why they didn't do more of the things they like to do. The answer is because of fear and ego calling the shots, telling you that you don't have enough, are not good enough, and you will not have enough for the future.

Don't be tricked by the ego keeping you enslaved in the current unhappy place in your life with no growth.

"How can the creator give you more when you are not grateful for what you have?"

Most people are unhappy in the moment and are racing toward the next moment to find happiness because they don't think they have everything they need and are not grateful for what they have.

Life is about having everything you need, not having everything you want.

Materialism is a mental disease designed to try to fill the hole in your soul. Awaken and find gratitude this moment for everything you have.

The oldest lesson people continue to learn is they didn't realize what they had until they lost it.

"If you trust and believe, you get what you need,
If you don't believe, you won't get to receive."

*B*elieving in something greater than yourself is an important part of becoming one with the universe. It is also overlooked during most people's journey toward finding fulfillment and happiness.

Without trust you will only find loneliness, fear, doubt and insecurity.

We have come to this planet to become part of the universe, not separate from it. Feeling separate from all that is on this planet is the job of the ego. The ego finds the moment and the universe most distasteful.

Awaken to the universe or a God of your understanding, not misunderstanding.

The only things you need to know about God and the universe are the unconditional love and humor found in both.

"Life doesn't happen to you, life happens for you."

A lot of people feel they are victims of the past because of unfortunate circumstances in their lives. This is completely normal in today's society because the ego loves to get people to attach titles to their life stories.

When we awaken and dare to look at things with spiritual eyes we can then realize that everything happens for a reason and maybe that reason is none of our business, or maybe it's one of the mysteries of life on this planet.

Dare to reverse the curse and begin to forgive all the hurtful or painful experiences in your childhood, teenage years, or adulthood. All of these things that happened to you made you the person you are today.

You were hand-picked by the universe to awaken and live a spiritual life. Every challenge is an opportunity for growth and happiness.

"There's a high price to pay for money."

Have you ever heard anyone say, "Money is the root of all evil."?

How can a piece of green paper with a picture of a dead president on it be evil? If this is the case, many people get up every morning and work very hard for this so-called evil. The truth is that green paper cannot be evil. What people are willing to do for it could be considered evil.

Instead of calling money "The root of all evil", how about making friends with your money? Wouldn't you rather have a friend in your pocket, bank account, or even under your bed, instead of evil?

Instead of saying you don't have enough or you need to keep making more money, try saying you are grateful for what you have.

The universe loves to reflect its light back to the gratitude holders.

"Truth is opening up your heart and your mouth; Humility is opening up your ears and closing your mouth."

*I*t has been said that the longest distance is from the mind to the heart.

We need to understand that everything going on inside of our heads is not always the truth. Remember, feelings are not facts.

What's going on inside your heart is the truth.

Try taking a step back and listen to what is going on inside your head and then coming out of your mouth.

If you are in the moment with positivity and gratitude, and you are smiling and talking about what's right with your day, feel free to skip to the next page.

Just because everyone is gossiping and slamming people in person and on the Internet, doesn't make it okay. Dare to stand in your power and don't get sucked into the he-said, she-said hurricane.

"The only thing we have to fear is our fear of fear."

*D*id you know that fear stands for "False Evidence Appearing Real"?

Dare to make a list of all your fears and share them with a spiritual advisor or a trusted friend on the path.

Once you have tangible evidence, you will then be able to see, with the help of someone, that you are simply suffering from conditioned responses from your past, or illusions of the future. The truth is more than likely you are okay right here and now.

The only thing that is wrong is what's going on between our ears, which can be a dangerous neighborhood.

"The best things in life are not things."

*D*id you know that what people want the most are not tangible things at all?

All people truly want love, kindness, respect, honesty, safety, belonging, and trust, just to name a few. These are the reality of what people want that money can't buy and all that really matters.

Money and material items come and go, and it is an illusion to believe that you can find true long-lasting happiness from them.

"If no-thing changes, no-thing changes."

ost people will get to a crossroad in life and are sick and tired but not willing to do anything positive about it.

Alcohol, drugs, shopping sprees, and serial dating will only complicate your life and create more suffering.

Dare to try to change one thing today to try to make your present situation better.

You have to be able to ask someone for help, because if you could have done it on your own you already would have.

Self-help and helping others less fortunate than you, are action words. Knowing and doing are two different entities.

Remember, if no-thing changes, no-thing changes. Doing the same thing and expecting different results is the true meaning of insanity.

"How many moments have you missed looking forward to other moments in the future?"

*D*id you ever notice your mind spends a lot of time in the past or in the future? Unfortunately it is considered normal behavior because everybody is infected with it to a point of epidemic proportions.

Try awakening to the moment and try to stay present.

See how living in the past or future is causing unhappiness, suffering, and addiction in many ways shapes, and forms.

" Try to stay spiritual through pain or gain, rise or demise."

*I*t's easy to be a spiritual warrior if all is going well in your life, with all the bills paid and a gangster roll in your pocket, but what about when you get a life challenge: you lose a job; your partner leaves you; there's a death in the family; or someone close to you is killed in combat. Can you remain calm and not let anger, fear, or jealousy call the shots in your life?

"When the going gets tough, the tough get going."

Drugs and alcohol can't help you. They will only make things worse. Ask for help and take suggestions.

"You'll know when you know, when you know."

A lot of people spend time in the future. What's going to happen in the future? These people haven't figured out that nobody can predict the future, not even the weather man.

Life is full of uncertainties. If you cannot accept uncertainties you will suffer from anxiety and fear. If, however, you can accept uncertainties, you change the energy of your life.

Make friends with the moment and as a result, the universe will surround you with magic and miracles.

"Just because you don't see the sun,
doesn't mean it's not there."

Many people suffer from depression because of learned mind viruses.

Conditioned responses from the past are compounded by emotional, physical and financial roller coaster rides you put yourself on.

Some people do have chemical imbalances which will require proper medication, not street drugs and alcohol, to restore them to a sense of balance. Medication alone, however, may not help.

Changing your mental status from negative to positive is a must, with help through groups, therapy, and self-help books. It needs to be a full-time, get-well time, in order to be successful.

Changing your thought patterns to what's right with your day instead of what's wrong with your day is a great start, continued by staying focused on the day and moment for progress.

"Some people say what you don't know "won't" hurt you. Others say what you don't know "will" hurt you."

"If ignorance is bliss", why aren't there more happy people in the world? The truth is information and wisdom are essential for happiness in order to awaken and remain awakened.

We all have built-in forgetters. We need constant reminders each day so we don't forget the important stuff, and we don't go back into a dark and negative state of being.

Dare to team together with spiritual warriors to remind each other that life is a gift and not to be taken for granted or to be endured.

We are here to find happiness, plain and simple.

"Put the gavel down, take the black robe off,
and try to stop judging."

If you asked most people if they would like to be judged, the answer would be no. Why then is it so easy for us to judge friends, family and people we don't even know?

One way of stop trying to judge others is to stop judging ourselves.

Just because others have judged us in the past does not mean we have to carry that judgement with us for the rest of our lives, especially if it were not true to begin with.

Being told we were stupid and would never amount to anything is no way to go through life believing such hurtful, negative remarks.

*"Have you ever noticed that there are
no luggage racks on a hearse?"*

When we are no longer here on earth, do you really want a list of all of your material wealth and financial portfolio on your headstone?

When we awaken and realize we can't take anything with us, and what really matters has nothing to do with stuff, life begins to transform around us.

If you asked all people's higher mind what they would really want on their headstone, they would probably say that they found happiness, were a good person, had some good friends who would do anything for them, and were loved unconditionally by at least one person.

"Conflict within yourself causes conflict with others."

Have you ever been aware of the constant dialogue going on between your ears? Check in with yourself and see if it is filled with fears, doubts, insecurities and chronic complaining about not having enough or not being good enough.

Only when we put the hammer down and stop beating ourselves up over the past or present situations we are in, can we then start replacing our thoughts and actions with positive affirmations.

Once we are at peace with ourselves, we will experience an energy shift which will allow us to experience peaceful relationships with others.

"Drinking alcohol doesn't drown your sorrows,
it only irrigates them."

One of the biggest misconceptions people have about alcohol is that just because everyone is drinking it, and it is legal to buy and consume in many places, that it is all okay.

Some people use it as a social lubricant and others use it to take the so-called edge off at the beginning, middle, or end of the day, while others use it chronically to kill their brain pain.

When you wake up in the morning after drinking alcohol the day before, you will probably be in more pain than the day before.

Take a step back and ask yourself if you would pour alcohol in your eye? If not, why then would it be okay to pour it into your stomach?

A lot of wise people have said that they have never seen a drink of alcohol make anyone a better person.

"We are conscious while we are awake, but are we awake, while we are conscious?"

Most people are conscious while they are awake, but are not awake while they are conscious. This is the job of the ego keeping people asleep to the moment where the magic of the universe lives.

The only reality there has ever been is the here and now. It has never not been the here and now. The ego will get the human to defend the fact that there is time, both past and future. This is only an illusion, however, when we were in the past, we were in the here and now, and when we will be in the future, we will be in the here and now. Past and future are only thought patterns in our head. This is how the ego stays alive by keeping us in the past and future.

The ego has no power in the moment, in fact it finds the moment most distasteful. That is why it is called the "Power of Now."

"Try to get out of your head and into your heart."

One more very important tool for happiness is to become aware of our mindless, obsessive, compulsive thoughts with which we are completely identified.

Anyone on a self-help spiritual journey can tell you that identification with our streaming thoughts will continue to cause unhappiness and discontentment.

When we take a step back and quiet the mind to listen to our hearts, that's when the magic of the universe can enter our lives and allow us to experience the real reason why we are here.

"There is no Wi-Fi in the forest, but there will be a better, faster connection for you."

*D*id you know before the modern day synthetic, technologically-advanced life we all now know, our ancestors lived in the forests and got everything they needed and more, all organically? They were connected to all things because they knew all things were connected to them.

There was no hoarding and planning for retirement, because they were living their life's purpose. There is no retiring from your life's purpose when you love living your life's purpose.

"Miracles happen every day. The only people who experience them are the ones who believe in them."

*D*id you know that we live on a living, blue, green planet surrounded by a sun and a moon that moves oceans and mountains?

Did you know that you already have won the most important lottery?

Your egg was picked out of two million other eggs so you could experience this amazing miracle called life.

Instead of focusing on the news, politics, stock market, and what store is having a two-for-one sale, dare to look a little closer at the world around you. Maybe there is more to life than pin numbers, taxes, social media and 401K plans.

"Xanadu is not a place, it's a state of mind."

Many people have heard of a Utopian place called Xanadu where all things will be perfect.

There will be peace on earth and all people will respect one another. This cannot happen because people believe this is something that can happen in the future. Since there is no such thing as the future, peace and respect must happen here and now.

Xanadu can only happen or take place here and now, and it must start with you.

Whatever is lacking in your life, begin to share these things with others around you. For example, if you feel like people don't respect you or your things, start respecting other people and their things.

Watch the magic of the universe respond to any of the things you think your life is lacking. The formula works the same under all circumstances.

"Did you ever wonder why the creator gave us two legs, one for falling and one for getting back up?"

*D*id you ever wonder why we have two legs?

On the road of life we encounter many obstacles, bumps, ditches, sharp corners, uphills, downhills and straightaways. All the obstacles are designed for spiritual growth. The ego will tell us that this is life dealing us a bad hand of cards, and things like this should not be happening to us. If the road were smooth all the time we would have no skills.

Spiritual warriors will not be kept down no matter how many times they fall. They will keep getting back up. If the spiritual warrior's road were easy, everyone would be on it.

"Know who you are before telling
someone who they are."

The ego loves to get us to "Judge a book by its cover" and condemn a person by their past. The truth is that most people don't even know who they are themselves, let alone tell someone else who they are.

The moment you catch yourself judging, dare to take a moment to find out what that person is like, or try to help that person out any way you can. Before you know it you will be surprised to discover that you have a lot more in common than you think.

"Try not to take things personally, even if it's personal."

One of the most important jobs of the ego is to make sure that you take everything personally while making it all about you, no matter what. In this way it makes sure that you have a lot of things to talk and complain about, and to make you feel disgruntled and discontent.

The ego's job is to make sure that we make it all about self. Another name for this is Selfishness.

The majority of times we tend to take things personally, and it usually doesn't even have anything to do with us. It only feels this way and remember, feelings are not facts.

Dare to take a step back the next time you are thinking about taking something personally, even if it is personal.

"You don't have to be healthy to be happy,
but you have to be happy to be healthy."

Many people think that you have to be in perfect health, with a proper height-to-weight ratio, have perfect abs, and a perfect profile to be happy. The truth is that nobody's perfect and you should accept the way you are here and now.

The most important tool for health is happiness. Choose happiness here and now and continue this process one moment at a time, one day at a time.

Before you know it people will be complimenting you on how healthy you are.

"Make prayer your first choice and not your last resort."

*S*ome people think that prayer is only something you do when you get into a sticky situation. It has been said to never underestimate the "power of prayer." Prayer is the ultimate wireless connection.

Have you ever woken up and prayed for a great day? Have you ever prayed to the spirit of the universe for help in the morning and throughout your day?

Dare to incorporate prayer into your daily living and watch the magic and miracles happen in your life. Remember, prayer is asking and meditation is listening.

It's a tough row to hoe thinking that you are in control of your life, and you don't need help from the spirit of the universe.

"Use your mind for mindfulness, not mindlessness."

id you ever become aware of the words coming out of your mouth? Are they positive or negative, helpful words or hurting words?

Did you ever become aware of what you were thinking about? Were they positive, grateful, healing thoughts, or were they self-destructive, vindictive, and jealous thoughts filled with resentments?

Dare to awaken to the moment full of mindfulness. See how consciousness and mindfulness will allow you to see if what you were thinking and saying is helping or hurting you.

Watch your thoughts because they become words. Watch your words because they become actions. Watch your actions because they become habits. Watch your habits because they become character. Watch your character because it becomes destiny.

*"Change your thinking and you will change your actions.
Change your actions and you will change your thinking."*

Unhealthy lifestyles often start out as a thought which then turns into speech, then into action. To try to change into more of a healthy lifestyle we must look at the core root of the problem which are mind viruses or fear.

To be willing to change, we must become aware of our negative thinking. Sometimes it takes a pretty painful situation to make us become willing to change.

"Like electricity we must be positive and grounded."

It is not by accident that to complete an electrical circuit there must be a positive and a ground. After all, we as humans are pure consciousness and energy. As energetic spiritual beings we too must have positivity and ground.

Until we become aware of our thinking patterns, we will not know if we are thinking positive or negative.

By being consciously aware of our positive thoughts and actions in each moment we are automatically grounded in the present.

By becoming aware that you are not in the moment, you automatically bring yourself back to the moment.

Congratulations! You have just become a Zen Master.

"The purpose of life is to live life with a purpose."

Many people have jobs that they don't like or maybe even hate, and spend most of their time thinking about this thing called "retirement." This is because they cannot accept the fact that whatever they are doing this moment is in fact, their life's purpose.

Most people will not change their current situation to find a new life's purpose because of fear of the unknown or feeling trapped in their current situation.

Dare to have faith and figure out what you would love to do each day. Then pray and put forth effort toward changing.

Wouldn't it be great to wake up in the morning and go to sleep at night smiling?

"If you do all the talking you will only learn what you already know."

A lot of people love to do all the talking out of unconsciousness, nervousness, ego, and self-centeredness. The ego loves to get Mr. and Mrs. Microphone to keep talking with mindless negative chatter so that it can try to stay in control.

See if you are able to listen to someone else speaking without obsessively and compulsively thinking about the next thing you are going to say because you believe it is more important. By doing this, you will actually be listening and caring about what the person is trying to say to you.

Try to find the "Energizer-Bunny" shut-off switch inside your brain, and try cutting out caffeine and alcohol.

"Don't betray the moment."

*O*nce we become aware that the only reality is the present moment, can we then begin the practice of keeping it in the moment. Everything else in the universe, with the exception of most humans' minds, is in the moment. Trees, plants and all animals are constantly in the moment. They don't have a choice. We as humans do have a choice, but most humans don't keep it in the moment. It's not that we are incapable, it's that we are unwilling.

Why not be where our feet are? Our body is always in the moment, so why not pair up with it, like Bluetooth, and experience the experience. Why not experience life in the moment? It's not as unpleasant or scary as we think it might be. If a moment comes that is unpleasant for us, instead of drifting and dreaming from the past into the future, dare to make a change by removing, changing, or accepting the situation as it is.

"Money is like cow manure, you have to spread it around for it to grow."

We have all heard the saying, "Save your money for a rainy day." Why can't we save it for a sunny day?

While spending money frivolously to try to fill the hole in your soul is never a positive thing, can't we open our mind, heart and wallet to help some charities and soup kitchens in your area. Give freely to the less fortunate people. Don't judge those who are helping or collecting, thinking they might have ulterior motives. The universe recognizes your generosity and kindness and will return the favor ten-fold.

The harder you try to hold onto your money, the more it will slip through your fingers like grains of sand.

"Nothing made fast is good. Nothing made good is fast."

We are currently living in a society where most humanity has been taken out of the equation and cast to the wayside, because of living in a fast-paced, multi-tasking environment.

Dare to take a step back and put your total focus and ethics into whatever you may be doing. Go the extra mile without expecting anything in return, and don't take any shortcuts.

Whenever you meet someone like yourself who is totally focused and doing a great job, make sure to compliment that person.

Everything you do in your life is important whether you believe it or not. Everything you do with consciousness and ethics will change how good your life will be. This is something that can't happen in the future. This is something that you can do now and find happiness now.

"You can't get there unless you are here.
Most people are not here because they are not all there."

$\mathcal{Y}$ou will hear many people say that they will look forward to this, that or another thing. When you look forward you are missing out on the moment in which you are living. This is the ego's way of keeping us out of the moment. Remember that happiness can only be found in the moment, so try to stop looking forward to happiness that can be found here and now.

The journey to the top of the mountain starts "here and now." There has only ever been "here and now." There will only ever be "here and now."

Remember, it is never not "here and now."

"Don't miss out on the moment taking pictures of the moment, so you can miss out on the moment looking back at the moment you missed taking pictures."

Every moment of life is precious. Choose wisely the way you spend each moment. You only get one chance to be present in each moment to enjoy life and every occasion in life.

Instead of running around taking pictures, try putting down the camera and be fully present experiencing the experience without doing anything.

Pictures cannot capture the energy and spirit that you will miss while taking the pictures. Instead, try hiring a professional photographer.

" Try not losing your head while others are losing their minds."

*I*t seems in today's society a lot of people have a hard time controlling themselves. Road rage, people screaming at each other, and domestic violence are some of the ways people are displaying the pressures of daily life in a fast-paced world. Anyone who has ever been involved with this type of behavior knows only too well that they don't help any of these conditions which are driven by fear.

Rather than reacting and allowing the road rage to live inside your head rent free, practice the art of non-reaction. In a very short period, the negative feelings will dissipate

*"If you are trying to control something,
it's already out of control."*

A lot of people try to jump on the addiction maintenance wagon out of fear because they have already experienced what happens when they overindulge. This includes food, shopping, sex, drugs, and alcohol. The truth is the maintenance program never works for long. It will always manifest itself back to the place and state of mind you don't want to be in.

Instead of doing the same thing expecting different results, try becoming aware of the core root of the addiction with the help of professionals and self-help groups. Admit that you should not be partaking in these activities. Whatever the affliction, there is sure to be help available, if you are willing to ask for it and want to change.

"Paradise is not a place in which you live,
but a place that lives within you."

Some people believe that happiness is found in a place. While it is true that a lot of places are beautiful, long lasting happiness will elude you. Geographical cures won't work because you will always bring yourself with you.

The ego wants you to believe happiness is found in a tropical vacation paradise. If you move there you might find happiness for a while until the old you shows its face. Paradise already lies within you.

If you would pause for a second, you will realize you are a miracle – "a diamond in the ruff." Paradise is found within you, the moment, and the universe.

"Believe in wisdom and life will be wisdomatic."

"Believe in magic and life will be magical."

"Believe in miracles and life will be miraculous."

"Believe in nothing and life will be lonely."

*A*s human beings we all need something to believe in. The ego wants us to be so-called self-sufficient and to depend only on ourselves. Maybe someone from the past has told you the big lie that you can only depend on yourself. How is that working out for you?

Part of being an open-minded, free-spirited, free thinker is that you can believe in anything your heart desires. There are many paths to enlightenment. If anyone tells you your path is the wrong path, run away from them as fast as you can.

"Don't let someone dim your Light simply because it's shining too brightly in their eyes."

A lot of people who dwell in the darkness despise "Light-Workers" simply because they are smiling and having a good day.

The darkness dweller will put a target on the light worker's back and try to ruin their moment any way they can. This is the time to amp up the flood lights and kill these people with kindness. These people have everything they need with the exception of love and kindness. These people may have had unspeakable acts done to them to make them who they are. The fact is, they are asleep to what they do and cannot be held responsible. Light workers must not dim their lights, but must have compassion for the unconscious ones.

"Denial ain't just a river in Egypt."

Have you ever wondered why it is so easy to see what's wrong with people's lives, but fail to see what's wrong with our own? This is called the disease of "Denial".

A famous person once said, "Why can we see the spot in our brother's eye, but fail to see the log in our own?" This is the ego hard at work, never wanting us to see what's wrong with us and what we have done.

The next time someone is telling you something you don't want to hear, like you are acting angry, childish, selfish, jealous, or dishonest, try taking a step back and practice non-reaction. Instead of instantly denying it, try to see through the other person's eyes. You just might awaken to the sneaky ego.

"The happiest people don't have the best of everything,
they make the best of everything they have."

*I*n the material and monetary world, people are taught to believe, "The more you have, the more happiness can be achieved." This can be confusing for a lot of people because it can feel good to receive a large sum of money or some big ticket material wealth. The problem is that the feeling doesn't last, nor does the money, so it is always followed by unhappiness if we are trying to find happiness in the material world.

Dare to become a spiritual warrior and enjoy what you have today. Try being grateful and make the best of what's going on around you here and now.

There is no known side effect for making the best of everything.

"Be like the proton of the atom, full of positivity even though surrounded by negativity."

*I*t can be difficult at first to stay positive in a world full of negativity. If the proton can do it, so can we.

When we stay positive even though surrounded by negativity, our energy field changes and we start encountering coincidences for our highest and best. We start attracting the right people, places, and things into our lives.

Stay consciously aware of your thoughts, speech, and actions, and watch the universe's protons kick into high gear for magic and miracles.

Fasten your seat-belt because you are in alignment for happiness.

"Don't be so poor that you can't afford to pay attention."

One problem that continues to plague modern society is the inability to single task and remain focused with an ethical, moral compass.

Returning to the way this country was many years ago, when people took their time and focused on honor and integrity must start with you. If you find that people around you are doing half-assed work at half-steam, ask yourself if you are part of the solution or part of the problem. Nobody likes poor quality work.

When you remain focused, practicing single-tasking, ethically and honorably, even though surrounded by people who do not, watch the universe reflect and reciprocate ten-fold.

"Greedy pigs have to sit in their own shit and are the first to go to slaughter."

ne of the seven deadly sins is greed. It seems in today's society that this is a widespread epidemic.

The ego tells us that we don't have enough, so we cannot be enough, and therefore we need to get out there and continue working like crazy because we don't think we have enough here and now.

Greed is the ultimate addict. No matter how much you feed it, it is never satisfied.

Dare to become aware of your greed. If you just thought to yourself that you are not greedy, congratulations! You have just been introduced to your ego.

"Everyone's been through hell; now it's your choice whether you choose to stay there or not."

*O*ne thing we can all say without a doubt is that on this journey of life sooner or later you will go through a difficult challenge and immense pain. This is the universal wake-up call to help pull you through the challenge and not stay consumed by it.

The ego loves to have us living in yesterday's traumas, dramas, issues and tissues.

The creator and your wise-minded higher self would like you to return to the present moment and find what's right with your day and not what's wrong.

" To strengthen your heart, the most important muscle in your body, try lifting someone's spirit.

A lot of people suffer from depression, caused by being consumed by self, and playing movies in their head of the traumas of yesterday. This is called the disease of mind. Instead, try to get out of your diseased mind and into your healthy heart.

Try helping a complete stranger or anyone you know that may have fallen on tough times. The ego hates when you commit a "Random act of kindness." There are no known side effects to "Random acts of kindness."

"It *ain't* odd, *it's God.*"

*O*nce awakened to the universe and all the positive energy that surrounds you, now will be the moment for all the coincidences or God moments to unfold right in front of your very eyes.

At first your response will be, "I can't believe it", followed by "I can believe it."

Staying in the moment, right here, right now, is why we are on this planet.

This is the reality. This is where the universe lives. This is where the Zen Masters live.

"We can't change the direction of the wind,
but we can adjust our sails."

*O*nce we realize that we can't control anyone or anything but ourselves, we end up sooner or later letting the universal light force drive the bus. We can then become the awakened spectator and passenger.

With the help of a spiritual-adviser we can make small incremental adjustments in our lives for our highest and best achievements. This will be a difficult task for most control freaks.

When we dare to turn it over and let the universe drive the bus we will feel the weight of our self-inflicted pain lifted off our shoulders.

"Forgiveness is a giver, resentment is a taker."

esentment runs rampant like an epidemic throughout most people's lives. Most people are unaware how much resentment lives inside their heads, causing toxicity. If you ask a lot of people if they have resentment in their lives, they will say, "no".

They may awaken and make a list longer than the one they once sent to Santa Claus.

Resentment robs us of precious energy and weakens our immune system. The remedy is forgiveness. Forgiveness does not mean what was done to us was okay. It means we will not let people, places, and things live inside our head "rent free".

"It's not what you do, but how you do what you do, that determines your destiny."

$\mathcal{U}$nderstanding the importance of everything we do and every move we make, is a big part of becoming conscious and awake.

Being ethical, having a moral compass, and doing the best job we can, pays big dividends with the universe. We don't do it to be rewarded , we do it to feel good and increase the positive flow around us.

All of these actions and mindsets create peace of mind, balance, and a great eight hours of sleep, which seem to be lacking in a lot of people's lives.

"Let your smile change the world, but don't let the world change your smile."

Have you ever noticed that most children at a certain age will greet you with a smile? After a period of time most will stop smiling and continue this into adulthood.

As an adult, try to become consciously aware, and reintroduce your smile into your day and to everyone you meet. Be like a friendly dog, happy to see everyone. You will begin to change your stagnant energy, and will start making people's days a lot easier, while making your own life better. Make sure you don't spend time with negative people and don't read the newspaper or watch the news so you don't relapse into your previous condition.

"There is no growth in the comfort zone, and no comfort in the growth zone."

Anyone who has tried to change and has become successful at it will tell you how difficult it was. This is why most people will not experience growth. They feel it is better to stay in the so-called comfort zone. If it were so comfortable, why would they be thinking about a change anyway? The truth is that it is uncomfortable at first when learning to change, followed by true freedom and growth.

Most people will give up trying to change due to fear of the new. Being only familiar with the old, people elect to be held hostage in their own self-made prisons.

Dare to ask someone or a group for help, and become the transformational spiritual alchemist you always wanted to be.

" The key to a simple life is to live life simply."

*I*n this technological complicated society, people's lives have also suffered complications. Simplicity has been cast to the wayside and most people don't think it is something to be revered and sought after. The truth is simplicity itself is genius.

People whose lives have become too complicated do not have enough time in the day and complain that everything is difficult. Such people cannot be happy at the same time.

Simplicity equals happiness. Dare to unplug. Relax in some humble surroundings.

"If you resist, it persists."

A lot of things that don't make sense when asleep will make perfect sense once awakened. These things are called paradoxes.

Some examples of paradoxes are:

"If you want to keep something, give it away."
"If you want to win, try surrendering."
"If you resist, it persists."

Most people will not accept what is happening in their lives right here and now. Job loss, divorce, sickness, financial problems and dysfunctional family issues are just some of life's challenges that people refuse to accept. The truth is, whether or not you accept what is happening, these things are happening. Only until you stop saying "these things should not be happening to me" and stop resisting what is, these challenges and situations are destined to continue.

"Fake it 'til you make it."

"Fake it 'til you make it" is a powerful tool to use when putting forth effort toward change. Most people are afraid to change or think they can't change.

When we make a decision to try to change, "Fake it 'til you make it" will help you make the transition.

When we begin to plant the seed of change in our mind and begin to believe it is possible for us to change, the brain will then release powerful chemicals to help you feel confident about your change. Before you know it, you will already be on the road to change. Once you have made the initial "Fake it 'til you make it", it will in fact become easier to implement more change into your life.

So, incorporate "Fake it 'til you make it" into your life and begin to notice how transforming your life by change leads to peace of mind and happiness.

"Happiness does not come from what you do,
Happiness flows into what you do."

Many people believe it is the activities that we do that bring us happiness. While no one can deny this has some truth to it, what good is it if it is followed by unhappiness? The truth is most activities allow happiness if we allow happiness to flow into all we do.

Happiness is achieved by living in the moment, accepting all that is, and staying connected to all that is.

Positivity and gratitude must be in the forefront of each moment, followed by not taking anything personal even when it seems or is personal. Try not minding what happens and be the "be" in human being, not a human doing.

We have come to this planet to awaken and find happiness in this moment no matter what is going on around us. If we do not achieve this, we will have to come back to this planet and do it all over again.

"The first sane thought you will ever have
is to admit you're insane."

Have you ever seen a homeless man sitting by himself, talking out loud to himself? Now pretend you put on some tattered clothing and go sit by yourself. Start saying out loud everything that's going on in your mind. There will not be a lot of difference between you and the homeless man except in reality you can control not saying some of what going on in your mind.

Instead of saying that other people are insane, become aware of the insanity in your own life. The ego will always justify your own insanity such as driving while texting, and operating a vehicle while under the influence of alcohol or drugs.

Become aware of your insane thinking, resulting in insane actions, and watch what happens to your life of chaos and anarchy. Sanity!

"Seeing is freeing."

Once we understand what is going on inside of us and we figure out why we did what we did, and why we do what we do, some powerful magic begins to happen. We begin to "see" for the first time in our lives whereas before we were asleep and blind.

The true magic happens when we begin to heal our old wounds by not letting fear and the ego call the shots in our lives. Don't let the fears and pains of yesterday interfere with our goal of happiness today.

The other powerful magic that happens is we understand others. We all have fears, doubts, and insecurities. Some have awakened and have become aware of them, while others remain asleep to them. Instead of knocking heads with the asleep one's, creating ego versus ego, have compassion for these people just like people had for you when you were asleep.

Final Thoughts

Be like the tree.

The tree stands tall, deeply rooted in the earth mother, sharing its roots with other trees.

The tree stays interconnected to all trees for strength.

The tree that stands alone is the tree that falls down.

The tree does not mind what color you are, what you have done in your past, or what God you believe in.

The tree will always welcome you in and provide you with shade.

The tree stays open each day and accepts each day as it has been written by the creator.

Whether hot or cold, sunny or cloudy, rainy or windy, the tree knows it needs all these elements to keep growing.

The tree is always in the moment and at one with the universe, because the tree knows we are all one tribe.

Be like the tree!

S. C. Klane

Made in the USA
Middletown, DE
12 September 2022

72747386R00055